published by Parragon in 2011

agon
en Street House
ueen Street
BA1 1HE, UK

BN: 978-1-4454-3849-8

Printed in China

Sav
Grac

First

Par
Que
4 Q
Bat

Co
De

Al
sy
r

Saving
Graces

a collection of inspirational thoughts and images

Bath · New York · Singapore · Hong Kong · Cologne · Delhi
Melbourne · Amsterdam · Johannesburg · Auckland · Shenzhen

Don't wait for the Last Judgment. It happens every day.

Albert Camus

Faith is a living, daring confidence in God's grace, so sure and certain that a man could stake his life on it a thousand times.

Martin Luther

Our greatest glory
is not in never falling
but in rising every
time we fall.

Confucius

A man travels the world over
in search of what he needs
and returns home to find it.

George Moore

In a gentle way,
you can shake
the world.

Mahatma Ghandi

Nothing in life is to be feared. It is only to be understood.

Marie Curie

To **know** the road **ahead,** ask those coming **back.**

To me, every hour
of the day and night
is an unspeakably
perfect miracle.

Walt Whitman

Give light
and people will
find the way.

Ella Baker

As we struggle

to make sense

of things, life looks

on in repose.

Anonymous

Don't **cry** because it's over.
Smile because it happened.

Dr. Seuss

In the middle of difficulty lies opportunity.

Albert Einstein

Do not **wait** for
your ship to come in -
swim out to it.

Anonymous

It's always
too early
to quit.

Norman Vincent Peale

What **matters** is not
the **idea** a man holds,
but the **depth** at
which he holds it.

Ezra Pound

Most men pursue pleasure
with such breathless haste
that they hurry past it.

Søren Kierkegaard

Stand at the crossroads, and look, and ask for the ancient paths, where the good way is and walk in it, and you will find rest for your souls.

Jeremiah 6:16

Fear makes the wolf bigger than he is.

German Proverb

Faith is taking the first step
even when you don't see
the whole staircase.

Martin Luther King Jr.

Gratitude is the fairest blossom which springs from the soul.

Henry Ward Beecher

A man who doesn't **trust** himself can never truly trust **anyone** else.

Cardinal de Retz

Resolve to be thyself;
and know that he who finds
himself, loses his misery.

Matthew Arnold

Hope is a
waking
dream.

Aristotle

It is never too late
to be what you might
have been.

George Eliot

Yesterday is history.
Tomorrow is a mystery.
And today? Today is a gift.
That's why we call it
the present.

Babatunde Olatunji

Fear knocked at the door.
Faith answered.

And lo, no one was there.

Anonymous

Do not seek to follow in the footsteps of the wise. Seek what they sought.

Matsuo Basho

Learn as if you were going to live forever. Live as if you were going to die tomorrow.

Mahatma Gandhi

If you can find a path
with no obstacles,
it probably doesn't lead
anywhere.

Frank A. Clark

Look at everything as though you were seeing it either for the first or last time.

Betty Smith

The best way to
succeed in life is
to act on the advice
we give to others.

Anonymous

It is a good divine that follows his own instructions.

William Shakespeare

It's not what you
look at that matters,
it's what you **see**.

Henry David Thoreau

The way to gain a **good** reputation, is to endeavor to be what you **desire** to appear.

Socrates

A problem is a chance for you to do your best.

Duke Ellington

A man can be
destroyed
but not defeated.

Ernest Hemingway

Do what you can, with what you have, where you are.

Theodore Roosevelt

To live is the rarest

thing in the world.

Most people exist,

that's all.

Oscar Wilde

The essence of pleasure is **spontaneity.**

Germaine Greer

No snowflake
ever falls in the
wrong place.

Zen

Reason is our soul's left hand,
Faith her right.

John Donne

Man is a being in search of meaning.

Plato

The awareness of our **strength** makes us modest.

Paul Cézanne

Faith is a living, daring confidence in God's grace, so sure and certain that a man could stake his life on it a thousand times.

Martin Luther

God will never give you
any problems that
he thinks you can't solve.

Og Mandino

Have a heart that never hardens,
a temper that never tires,
a touch that never hurts.

Charles Dickens

Picture credits